THE
Archive Photographs
SERIES

HORNSEA

On top of the world here at Hornsea.

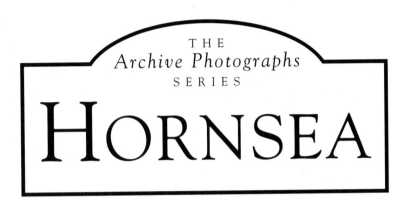

THE
Archive Photographs
SERIES

HORNSEA

Compiled by
G. L. Southwell

CHALFORD

First published 1995
Copyright © G. L. Southwell, 1995

The Chalford Publishing Company
St Mary's Mill, Chalford,
Stroud, Gloucestershire, GL6 8NX

ISBN 0 7524 0302 8

Typesetting and origination by
The Chalford Publishing Company
Printed in Great Britain by
Redwood Books, Trowbridge

Contents

Acknowledgements

The author wishes to acknowledge the help and assistance generously given by the following in the preparation of this book.

F.W. Banks, Mrs E. Bradley, W.J.C. Browning, Mrs S.M. Buttimer, G. Hood, The *Hull Daily Mail*, Hornsea Museum, V.M. Kirwan, M.J. Lonsdale, Mrs B.M. Parker, C.B. Rawson, M. Read, G.F. Southwell, Mrs I.M. Southwell, R. Thorndyke, W.E. Underwood, M.B.E.; Dr and Mrs J.E.S. Walker, M.G. Wood.

Hornsea *Domesday Book* entry. 'In Hornesse, Morcar had 27 carucates of land, and there might be as many ploughs there. Drogo now has there one plough, and Wizo his vassal one plough and nine villeins, and three bordars with one plough and a half. There is a church and a priest, and sixty acres of meadow … '.

Introduction

Hornsea is a small seaside town situated half way between Bridlington and Spurn Point in the plain of Holderness, which is in the East Riding of Yorkshire. To the east lies the forbidding North Sea; to the South, the wide estuary of the river Humber, and in the West all roads to the East Riding must cross the fast flowing tidal river Hull. Being surrounded on three sides by water gives this part of Holderness a feeling of isolation.

The photographs in this book tell the story of Hornsea. The ancient settlement of Hornsea is mentioned in *Domesday Book*, which records the village as a valuable property. From its early days Hornsea was a settled village, which gradually grew into today's thriving town. The street pattern shows the town's ancient origins; the streets and lanes around the Parish Church suggest centuries of occupation, and their names tell their own tale: Westgate, Market Place, Southgate, Eastgate, the narrow lanes that lead from the Market Place to the Mereside and the quaintly named Back Southgate and Back Westgate, all add testimony to Hornsea's long past.

During the eighteenth century Hornsea became a popular watering place. The increasing number of visitors who came to enjoy the sea bathing and take the waters of the mineral springs, created a demand for accommodation and facilities unheard of in earlier times. Families moved their entire households to Hornsea for the summer and local residents provided accommodation for the visitors, thus adding to the new-found prosperity of the town.

All this activity was given a tremendous boost when, in 1864, the Hornsea railway to Hull opened, providing a direct link to Hull and connections to the rest of the country. Now visitors could travel in style and the long tedious journey by horse and carriage was replaced by the comfort which the railway company offered. This same company built the ill-fated Pier at Hornsea. These changes set the seal for the expansion of the town during the next fifty years or so. New streets and new houses great and small were built. The Esplanade, Headlands View and Cliff Road were added to the street pattern of this newly emerging seaside resort.

Fortunately, this period coincided with the invention and the rapid improvement of photography, which has allowed us to follow the development of Hornsea using the pictures in this book. We can see how the old has blended with the new to make today's modern town. These photographs, chosen from the author's extensive collection, are intended only as a glimpse of the fascinating world of yesteryear. Hornsea is a much photographed place and so much material is available that the task was what to leave out rather than what to include.

The Hornsea of today provides plenty of recreation and amusement, the tradition of involvement in the social life of the town is strong and annual events such as the Music Festival, the Speech and Drama Festival, the Carnival and the Christmas Lights provide plenty of diversion each year.

In this book the reader is taken first on a journey through the town starting in Westgate, the principal road into the town from the west. Westgate, Market Place and the streets and the lanes of the old town are shown. The old and the new views show the changes that have taken place. From the town the scene changes to the Parish Church and Hall Garth Park. This park is is not a formal Victorian park, but one of natural beauty lying alongside the town. The Mere, Yorkshire's largest area of freshwater, now a bird sanctuary accessible to the public, has been sensitively managed giving an exclusive feature to Hornsea that is the envy of many.

No tale of Hornsea would be complete without pictures of the railway. The Hull to Hornsea line lasted from 1864 until 1964, just one hundred years. In the limited space available in this book the few pictures of the Railway can hardly do justice to such an important undertaking. The scene changes to the seafront, showing the days before the sea wall and promenade were built when the Pier and the bathing machines provided visitors with their recreation; from there to Edwardian Hornsea and the Floral Hall, with the new Promenade and seaside amusements all familiar to the pleasure seeking crowds arriving here on the bank holiday excursion trains.

The book shows the people of Hornsea at work and play, also the world famous Hornsea Pottery which played a significant part in the life of the town from the early days when the Rawson brothers first began to produce their distinctive ware in the mid fifties. The next section features the children showing schooldays and holidays alike.

Last, but by no means least, the military. Hornsea's strategic position on the coast has meant that over countless centuries this part of Yorkshire has attracted the Armed Forces. The pictures in this book show the passing phases of Military activity both in war and in peace. The story ends with a farewell said for us by a young visitor enjoying his holiday on Hornsea's beach.

One
Westgate, Market Place and Southgate

Hornsea from Kirkham Point on the Mere.

This attractive building on Seaton Road was erected as a school by Lady Constable in the 1830's and included accommodation for the teacher. Today it is a most attractive dwelling-house beside one of the busy main roads into Hornsea.

A dozen or so schoolchildren play on the grass verge outside the infants' school, a hundred years after it was built. No kerbstones or tarmacadam yet! This school closed when the new school opened in Newbegin in 1936.

This picture was taken some forty years later and shows the group of buildings at the junction of Seaton Road and Westgate.

This is the western entrance to Hornsea. Westgate passes to the left of Stanley Lodge and Back Westgate to the right. The imposing frontage of the Pillars with the two mature trees and cobbled pavement add elegance to the view. The Pillars was for many years a private school.

A Carnival procession in Westgate some time during the 1920's. The fancy dress costumes delight the spectators whilst babies and older folk enjoy the sunlit parade. It is interesting to look at the appearance of the people in the crowds, particularly the hats, gloves, and footware – to say nothing of the bicycles, prams, and horse-drawn vehicles.

Just a few yards further along from the previous picture, Sunset Cottage shows clearly the white-washed cobble walls and pantiled roof of a typical local cottage. Two unevenly placed dormer windows have been added at a later date. Cottages built in this traditional way were once a regular feature of Hornsea.

This picture leads into the western end of the Market Place. The view, taken from a painting, is dated around 1824 and clearly shows an open air market taking place. All the buildings in the picture can still be identified today. The gates of the Old Hall on the left are next to the blacksmith's workshop (see page 42). St. Nicholas' Church tower appears on the sky-line as it looked before the renovations by the late Sir Gilbert Scott in 1876. Overlooking the Market Place is the face of the earlier Church clock.

Older inhabitants refer to this as the 'Bull Ring'. Legend has it that bull baiting took place at this end of the Market Place. This may have been so, but here the Bull Ring and its tree serve to separate the traffic at the junction of Westgate, Eastgate and Market Place. The scene is still readily identifiable after more than half a century has passed. Now traffic is controlled by a roundabout. The postcard is incorrectly named 'Newbigin'.

14

Henderson's shop in 1913 (postmarked) advertised the following newspapers: *Weekly Herald, Weekly Post, Picture Paper, Telegraph, Morning News, Yorkshire Herald, Daily Mail, Daily Mirror, Weekly Telegraph* and *The Leeds Mercury*. The news headlines were: Bank Holiday Football; Coracles used in Salmon Fishing; Easter Football; How the World spent Easter Monday; Hundreds Killed in Storms; Suffragettes; Cottingham Show; Shocking fatality in Hull; and Devastating Cyclone in America. Also advertised were Robin Starch, Brasso, and Ogden's Guinea Gold Tobacco.

Built in 1864, the Methodist chapel occupies a strategic position at the western end of the Market Place. A few years ago the Chapel became derelict and was in turn a snooker club and a block of flats. Now by good fortune it has been returned to its former use and is once again a place of worship. The cannon under the tree is a reminder of wars past.

Looking south from the Market Place, Mr. Parker's shop is easily recognised by its distinctive curved window. He was a Provision Merchant, Baker and Grocer, and his shop provided the people of Hornsea with essential and luxury foods for many years. The children stop and stare in wonder at the camera man and his magic box.

Market Place & Market Cross, Hornsea

This is Hillerby Lane which leads from the Market Place to Mereside. Most of these cottages have been demolished but some traces of the cobble walls remain. The two young boys propel their bogie (made from a set of old pram wheels) down the gentle slope of the lane towards the swings and roundabout on the green at Mereside.

Opposite: This row of shops is opposite the market cross which nowadays stands in the churchyard. From left to right: A. C. Tabors, Jewelry; Wheldale, Tobacconist; Hornsea Pottery Shop; Argenta, Butchers; Yorkshire Electricity Board; and Smiths, Pork Butchers Shop. Above the shops is the art department of the Hornsea Pottery Co. Behind the big tree, just in view, is a small road-roller. This photograph was taken in the early 1950's. Today this is still a very busy road junction controlled by traffic lights and a pedestrian crossing.

The junction of Southgate, Newbegin and Market Place. This is another view of Mr. Parker's Stores. The three-storeyed building in the background is the New Inn which is now called the Pike and Heron. The names above the shops can be seen clearly as can the narrow passage between the Central Stores and Loten Bros., chemist's shop. This passage is called Mere Walk and leads to Mereside. There is a donkey and cart parked just on the corner. At least three of the shops have tall flag poles.

Almost the same view, but what a difference! Children, housewives, workmen, shop assistants, builders and their mates on the roof, ponies and traps and warmly clad ladies all looking up at the camera man. The shops are open for business and it is a working day. What were all these folk doing on this wintry day?

Southgate looking towards the Market Place. A busy scene in the 1920's shows fashionable ladies out shopping, the open-topped touring car in the centre of the road, the child on his tricycle, the delivery boy on his bike. There are advertisements for Ingersoll watches and further down for Royal Daylight Oil (paraffin). There is just one wall-mounted gas street lamp at this end of Southgate.

A group of buildings in Southgate replaced by Pybus Court, a block of flats for the elderly. The front of the two storeyed building collapsed into a trench whilst work was being carried out on underground cables. The house was demolished and the occupant rehoused in a much safer building.

This corner of Southgate changed with the demolition of the once popular Lill's fish and chip shop on the right hand side in this picture. After closing time the shop did a roaring trade as homeward-bound drinkers called in for their fish and chip suppers.

The Wednesday Market Cross outside the Cemetery Chapel in Southgate, 1913. This cross is reputed to have belonged to the village of Hornsea Burton, lost to the sea. The two ladies cycle carefully past the row of cottages, which in later years made way for the Catholic Church. In the distance, under the trees, comes the horse-drawn water cart spraying the dry roads to 'slake the dust'. Outside the farm gates the small boy has just collected the family's milk in a milk can.

This handsome building, known variously as Low Hall or White House Farm, has a long history. At one time it belonged to the Quaker family of Acklam and there is a Quaker burial ground adjacent to the farm. Beyond the cobble wall is the main public entrance to the Mere. The Old Mission Hall and Lill's fish and chip shop can be seen in the distance.

In 1962 a major road widening scheme was carried out in Southgate between the Wednesday Market Cross and the junction with Hull Road. There was a general clearance of the buildings on the east side of the road. This is Stonehouse Farm, also known as Bank's Farm, just prior to demolition in October 1962. Modern bungalows now occupy this site.

Round the corner from Stonehouse Farm is the building once used by Peter Beckwith for his taxi business. Here the taxi is parked outside the office. Behind the taxi office the exposed roof timbers of the partly demolished house show up in the winter sunshine. It is about here that Stream Dyke passes under Southgate carrying the overflow from the Mere to the sea.

Two
Eastgate and Newbegin

Corner Cottage stands where Eastgate begins. Mill Lane leads away to the left past the tall, narrow building that was once Mr. Barr's Joiners shop. A tall chimney stood near the workshop as part of the steam engine used to drive the machinery. The small paned workshop window made from random pieces of glass was an economical way of using an expensive and vulnerable material.

This most attractive cottage lies opposite the Eastgate entrance to the Hall Garth Park. Its cobble and pantile construction is typical of the district and uses local materials. It was to this cottage that T.E. Lawrence came as a visitor during his time in the Royal Air Force. He was then stationed at Bridlington under the name of Aircraftsman Shaw. It is said he looked for peace and solitude during his weekends here. Lawrence died following a motorcycle accident in 1935.

A peaceful scene in Eastgate. The trees on the grass verge are still an attractive feature today. The children so carefully posed in the picture could possibly be from one of the many private schools that existed in Hornsea at the time. Eastgate was one of the two old routes to the sea. In medieval times a gate led to the East Field, which lay to the north of the town and was farmed in common by the townsfolk. Hornsea was enclosed under an Act of Parliament passed in 1801, the award being dated 1809. The effect of this Act was to improve the agriculture, drainage and roads in the Parish, and this helped to prepare Hornsea for the many changes that were about to take place.

The rural, tree-lined character of Eastgate continues here and is still much in evidence today. The houses behind the fence on the left overlook Hall Garth Park.

Eastgate in the 1870's, looking down the hill towards Cliff Lane. At the bottom of this hill the land was very wet and boggy in winter and there is evidence that the road used to follow the line of the high ground where the present-day hospital stands, then curved back towards the sea. As drainage improved, the boggy bits dried out and Eastgate followed the line it does today. Modern Eastgate makes a junction with Ashcourt Drive just here and behind the trees is the large house called Burnside.

Here Eastgate crosses Cliff Road and continues on its way towards the sea front. Between here and the sea it is known locally as Little Eastgate. The broken white line markers on the road seem strangely quaint when compared with the complex markings of the present day junction. This car driver still has the habit of early drivers, they occupied the centre of the road!

Two characters pose for a photograph outside the Lodge in Eastgate. William Shipley from Driffield, who owned this car, also owned the steam roundabout at Hornsea which appeared regularly, providing seaside entertainment for the visitors. His passenger is Miss Rose Carr, who died in 1913, a lady who led a busy life as a carrier and horse dealer. Rose Carr's exploits are well documented in the Hornsea Museum.

This is how most people like to remember Eastgate, as a shady tree lined thoroughfare. The dappled sunlight shows up the sandy surface of the road and serves as a reminder that we enjoy a much higher standard of road surfacing today. Here the cobble wall has been breached to allow a house to be built on the south side of the road overlooking Hall Garth Park.

Now back to the centre of the town where Newbegin joins the Market Place. This is how Newbegin looked in the 1860's. The Market Cross stood in the centre of the road. The cottages on the left (now demolished) stood between the churchyard and the street. The buildings on the right-hand side are familiar today. The first major road widening scheme is about to take place.

The demolition of the houses by the church and the removal and repair of the cross were part of Hornsea's first important road widening scheme. The cross was renovated and re-erected in the churchyard. This picture was taken just before the unveiling and re-dedication ceremony, part of Queen Victoria's Diamond Jubilee celebrations on 6 July 1898.

Moments later and the restored, re-furbished market cross, whose secular use was to mark the Monday market granted in 1275, has been blessed. It now stands in the corner of the churchyard of St. Nicholas' Church overlooking the new road junction. The ceremony is watched by a crowd representative of the local inhabitants.

This picture, taken during the 1960's from the same point as the one on page 29, shows the changes that have taken place in a hundred years. The road is wider and has a tarmacadam surface with road markings. There are no houses in front of the church and the trees that were behind the houses are now near the pavement. Street lighting and motor traffic have become commonplace. Most of the buildings on the right have been replaced by shops.

A fine picture of Newbegin near Bank Street. The row of buildings next to the Bank are worth a close look. Beyond the house next to the bank is an old, single-storeyed building which was at one time a chapel, then a dwelling. For some years now it has been a cafe. Next comes a row of shops built in pairs. They share the same roof line and in spite of later additions it is possible to see the original construction and design. On the left is Burns Farm which is now the Hornsea Museum. In the distance along the central part of Newbegin there has been a great deal of demolition and re-building which has once again changed the face of the Town.

Central Newbegin before the major alterations took place. The cottages on the left are where Rose Carr lived and worked. She kept a variety of horses and ponies ready for work in her stables. Her cottage was called Tea Tree Cottage because of the tea tree bushes which can be seen growing in front of the building. All the buildings on the left have been demolished and replaced by shops.

These are the cottages on the left in the previous picture. Rose Carr is standing outside her office. She lived here until her death in 1913. From here she ran her successful carrier business. Her life and times are recorded in a book published locally. She made her mark in many ways and was once reported as having been fined, along with fellow carrier Lamplough Potter, for driving her waggon in a reckless and furious manner on the highway. No trace of any of these buildings can be found today.

Newbegin, February 1947. Most people who can remember the end of the Second World War will remember the winter of 1947. The snow fell and remained until March was over. In the distance the milkman, Jim Hartley, is delivering his milk as he did every day whatever the weather.

Newbegin is marked at one end by the church of St. Nicholas and at this end by the Congregational Church. Around here are some of the important municipal buildings of the town. On the left, by the flag pole, is the Police Station, and the Wesleyan Chapel built in 1875. Beyond the Chapel and out of sight are the Public Rooms. Then comes the Congregational Church, later the Reformed Church. The Churches have maintained their original purpose whilst the other buildings in the group have either changed use or have been demolished.

Newbegin in the 1860's, taken from the end looking west towards the Parish Church. On the left is one of the village pumps that provided drinking water before the Municipal water works were built. Farm buildings and small cottages predominate. The small boys in this picture would be astounded if they could see the scene today with a busy school crossing and supermarket dominating the area.

Newbegin ends here! Newbegin is described elsewhere as extending some three hundred yards more or less from the Market Place towards the sea. It is here that the half-way mark between Hornsea and the sea is noticeable. Ahead lies Cliff Lane running parallel to the sea for about half a mile. To the right is New Road with terraces of imposing Victorian houses leading down to the sea. The sunblind is down on Loten Bros. chemist's shop. The delivery van waits by the roadside and the little girl on the cart has a smile for the camera.

Three

The Church and Hall Garth Park

Both St. Nicholas' Church and Hall Garth Park appear in this attractive picture taken from Eastgate. Behind the trees on the extreme right is the Old Hall. The middle ground is taken up with the expanse of the Park. The cobble wall is still there but the archway has disappeared. The construction of a cobble wall is shown clearly here. The majority of the cobbles would have come from the beach, having been washed out of the cliffs, and include many varieties of stone.

This aerial view of St. Nicholas' Church includes a good view of the white walled Vicarage. Newbegin runs along the front of the church and then turns into the market place. In the upper part of the view can be seen two holes of the nine hole golf course in the park. The church is almost surrounded by a screen of mature trees.

This new clock mechanism was fitted in the church to commemorate the men who fell in the Great War. It was made by G.J.F. Newey of York and installed in the tower in 1921. At the same time the peal of bells was increased from three to eight and a keyboard fitted. The previous clock had only one face; the new one has a face on three sides of the tower. The additional bells make it possible for the clock to chime hours and quarters and for hymns to be played on the bells.

St. Nicholas' church on a quiet morning near Christmas. The Christmas tree, a gift from the local Chamber of Trade, is illuminated, and a collecting box stands on the wall by the tree. The early winter sun highlights the variety of texture and colour in the fabric of the church. The Victorian wrought iron railings were removed from the church wall and taken for scrap metal to aid the war effort. This opened up the southern aspect of the church.

From the tower of the church looking north-east over the open space of the park. Hall Garth Park came into the possession of the Hornsea Urban District Council in November 1919. The land had previously belonged to the Constable family of Wassand. The area is of about 20 acres, 2 roods or thereabouts, and was known as Old Garth. It was probably part of the 60 acres of meadow that was mentioned in the *Domesday Book* entry for Hornsea.

A fine picture taken at the seaward end of Newbegin from the top of the Congregational Church, looking out over the roofs of the coastguard cottages. In the centre is another carefully tended green on the golf course. In later years an 18 hole course was built on Rolston Road. The large detached house just below the horizon is Burnside in Eastgate, where Winston Churchill stayed during his inspection visit on 31 July 1940.

The magnificent 'Alphabet' gates that grace the Cliff Road entrance to Hall Garth Park were a gift to the people of Hornsea from John Hollis of Mill House. John Hollis was a well known Hull timber merchant who came to live in Hornsea. The wrought iron gates were installed in 1929. They were made by Chris Burton in his blacksmith's shop in the market place. The gates bear the legend "Enter Hall Garth with title free, You'll find your name is wrought on me".

Chris Burton at work in his blacksmith's shop in 1929. It was here that the Hall Garth Park gates were made. All the working tools are arranged around the walls. The smith is heating a horse shoe in the forge ready to work it into shape on the anvil.

Four

The Mere
and the Railway

Looking westward from the church over the Mere, the largest stretch of fresh water in Yorkshire. Nowadays it is a bird sanctuary and a recreation area. Hornsea Mere is the last of many meres that were once a feature of Holderness.

The Mere offers fine sailing. Here, in 1950, a Hornsea 15 leads the field to win in a brisk force 6-7 wind. At the helm is Gordon Hood with crewman Bill Banks out of sight behind the foresail. These two young men later became the proprietors of the fishing and boating facilities at the Mere.

On Hornsea Mere, 1948. A group of three boats at anchor. The white hull is *Niad*, the yawl is *Kittywake* and the third is *Freak*. In the background behind the houses is the site of the Hornsea Gas Works, the retort chimney is just visible over the rooftops. The gas works have long gone, replaced by the supply of North Sea Gas.

The spectators at the Association of North Eastern Yacht Clubs open meeting held at Hornsea Mere in 1950. A good stiff breeze made for a lively event and the competitors have caught the audience's attention. In most crowd pictures there is usually a dog and a small boy – this is no exception.

Hornsea Mere. The handle of the landing net bends to the weight of the pike, just caught on rod and line by the fishermen. Generations of fishermen have fished the Mere from the bank or from a boat. Careful control of the fishery has ensured that the lake has remained well stocked with a variety of coarse fish.

Hornsea Mere 1946. On the left is the Norwegian built *North Star* and on the right *Ilex*. *Ilex* was evacuated to the Mere from Brigham for the duration of the war !

The one that didn't get away! A 25-pound pike caught from a boat on the Mere. The fisherman has the essential tools of his hobby on the thwart, a bait tin, a tackle tin, a box of sandwiches and a flexible rule to measure the catch.

Hornsea Mere, 1938. A Short Singapore III on the Mere, one of a flight of these military flying boats that tested the Mere for use as an operational base should war make it necessary. Fortunately for Hornsea the idea was dropped, otherwise Hornsea would have been a prime target for the Luftwaffe in later years. The Mere has a long association with seaplanes and flying boats, which will be the subject for a later book.

Hornsea Mere, 1906. In the days of our youth the winters seemed colder and the Mere froze more often. On this occasion the continuous hard frost meant that the ice was thick enough to support the weight of hundreds of people. The message on the reverse side of this postcard reads, ' Dear Edie, Thanks for your postcard, how do you like this one? It was taken a fortnight ago. Can you find me on it and don't you think I look well on skates? Hope you are all well, Love Jennie.'

The Railway, 1906. It must have been a very cold winter for the flooded fields down by the seaside station to have frozen hard enough to provide a skating rink for this crowd of skaters. Small wonder that many of Hornsea's older folk can ice skate. In the background is Hornsea Town signal box. The water crane and the water tower with its unusual horizontal windmill pump, share the scene with the steam and the smoke from a stationary locomotive.

Near the Hornsea Bridge station and goods yard a group of players take their recreation seriously. All the players are in fancy dress. The bewigged wicket keeper and uniformed batsman take their stance at the wicket, whilst the square leg umpire keeps his eye on the batsman. The two slips appear ready for action. Passengers and railway workers alike are showing a great interest in the game.

50

C. J. SELWAY
PASSENGER MANAGER

TELEPHONE BISHOPSGATE 7600
EXTENSION 2378
TELEGRAPHIC ADDRESS
"PASSENGER, C/o EASTLIN, LONDON"

REFERENCE

E.8/N/23-3

Letters to be addressed

THE PASSENGER MANAGER (SOUTHERN AREA)
LONDON & NORTH EASTERN RAILWAY
LIVERPOOL STREET STATION
LONDON E.C. 2

23rd March, 1939.

Madam,

In reply to your letter of the 21st instant, I have pleasure in quoting below details of the required train service from Hornsea to King's Cross, via Hull:-

MONDAY, 10th April.

	am	pm
Hornsea......dep.	10.37.	2.45
Hull (Paragon)arr.	11.20	3.29
" " dep.	11.55	5. 5
Doncaster (Cen)		
arr.	1.19	-
" " dep.	2.13	-
King's Cross..arr.	6.28	9.42

Page 12
Page 20

The enclosed Monthly Return ticket programme gives particulars of the Monthly Return ticket facilities from King's Cross to Hornsea.

Yours faithfully,
for C.J.SELWAY,
Passenger Manager.

Miss I.A.Gooding,
64, High Ridge Road,
HEMEL HEMPSTEAD. Herts.

Tickets may be obtained in advance by forwarding a remittance to this Office, together with full particulars of your requirements and quoting the reference shown; Cheques, Money Orders and Postal Orders should be made payable to "The London and North Eastern Railway Company," and crossed.

A courteous and informative letter from C.J. Selway to Miss I.A. Gooding, a potential passenger from Hornsea to King's Cross. The letter was written on 23 March 1939. The journey would take about eight hours but that would include waiting time at Doncaster. Those were the days!

A fine view of the main platform at Hornsea Town station. Just round the corner to the left the level crossing allowed the locomotive to run into the shunting neck and so run round the coaches to head the train back to Hull. The Alexandra Hotel stands in Railway Street. In later years the top storey was removed, altering the entire look of the building.

A group of travellers waiting on the main platform at Hornsea Town station. They find the time to have their photograph taken, perhaps as a memento of their holiday, perhaps as a family group before parting. The platform canopy covered most of the main platform, so passengers could board or leave the train in comparative comfort.

The railway in better days – Hornsea Bridge station. The railway line crossed the road on this bridge. Access to the station platforms was by flights of steps to both the up and down lines. There was no footbridge for passengers to cross the line. Signals on the gantry show a clear road on both up and down lines. The girl in the foreground is Dolly Capper.

Hornsea Town station during the last days of steam; No. 67371 British Rail tank engine with a full head of steam waits for the guard's signal. The children are shown the footplate under the benevolent eyes of the driver and fireman. The head code lamp by the funnel signifies a stopping train.

The Railway, 1962. A few years before the closure of the line, this Diesel Multiple Unit waits for the signal to start. There are no small children to admire the locomotive as there were in the previous picture. On a dull wet day the station platform and buildings show up clearly.

After the line closed completely the track was lifted and equipment removed or demolished. This was the fate that awaited the water tower at the Town Station. Sam Allon's swinging weight made short work of the water tower.

The end of the Hornsea Railway bridge. No longer needed, no longer required, redundant structures are demolished or removed. The mini van passes beneath what is left of the railway bridge. Within a short space of time the bridge had completely disappeared and now nothing is left of Hornsea Bridge Station. The posters on the bridge abutments advertise a United church service and sheep dog trials.

Five

Buildings

This aerial view of Hornsea shows the old pier head on the beach in the lower part of the picture. Behind is the Town Railway Station and above the station are streets of late Victorian houses. Across the two open fields are Mereside and the parish church; then the length of Hall Garth Park to the Congregational Church and New Road leading back to the sea. Most of the photographs in the book were taken within this area.

The Primitive Methodist chapel at the west end of the Market Place was built in 1864, the year the railway arrived. The Chapel served its congregations well for over one hundred years. Latterly it became a snooker hall, then was divided into flats and became derelict for a while. It was subsequently re-furbished and re-dedicated as a place of worship and is steadily regaining its original splendour. The circular memorial window disappeared for some years during the alterations but was found and has been restored and replaced.

Primitive Methodist Church, HORNSEA.

Sunday, Jan. 16th, 1910,

Special Mission Services at 10-30 and 6-30.

MISSIONERS: MESSRS.

Willis & Holland

AFTERNOON AT 2-30—

SACRED CONCERT.

Chairman: ... MR. W. TONG, Goxhill.

Programme:

OPENING HYMN.   PRAYER.

CHORUS	... ...	"The Summerland"	... ...	PARTY
SOLO	... ...	"The Holy City"	...	MR. HOLLAND
CHORUS	... ...	"View the Land"	... ...	PARTY
SOLO	... ...	"Calling the Prodigal"	...	MR. WILLIS
SOLO	... ...	"I heard the Voice"	...	MR. HOLLAND
CHORUS	... ...	"Just the Same"	... ...	PARTY
DUETT	... ...	"He Knows" ...	MESSRS. WILLIS & HOLLAND	
CHORUS	... ...	"Rocks and Mountains"	... ...	PARTY
SOLO	... ...	..."Side by Side" ...	...	MR. HOLLAND
CHORUS	... ...	..."A Meeting Here To-Night"	...	PARTY

SILVER COLLECTION.

MONDAY, JAN. 17th, MISSION SERVICE at 7-30.

On TUESDAY, Jan. 18th, MR. WILLIS
will deliver his

THRILLING LECTURE:

"From Tap-room to Pulpit."

CHAIR TO BE TAKEN AT 7-30.   SILVER COLLECTION.

To be followed by a COFFEE SUPPER, Tickets 6d. each.

ORGANIST:—MISS ANNIE ROBINSON.

E. Kemp, Printer, Grosvenor View, Hornsea.

A sample of the busy programme of events offered by the Primitive Methodists in their chapel.
This is an advertisement for an extensive programme of events for three days in 1910.

This double fronted shop is still in business in Newbegin today, and although now occupied by two businesses it is still recognisable as the large General Drapers shop once occupied by H. Stephenson (late W.R. Pearson). Note the advertisement for 'Daisy Vacuum Cleaners' and the wide assortment of goods on display.

Annual Clearance Sale.

SATURDAY, Feb. 8th to WEDNESDAY, 18th, 1908.

When in addition to **Great Reductions** in Goods out of Season, many every day requirements will be offered at **Special Prices.**

W. R. PEARSON,

Drapery, Millinery, Carpet, fancy Goods and furnishing Warehouse,

HORNSEA.

In 1908 Pearsons advertised their annual clearance sale with the aid of this postcard. These sales cleared the shelves of stock in time for the arrival of the new season's latest goods. The sale went on for just ten days.

The bicycle was once an important means of transport for work or play and was part of every day life. Its maintenance and replacement was an important part of a family's budget. Here, in 1908, a selection of cycles is displayed for sale outside Mr. Johnson's shop in the Market Place.

Mr. Barr's shop in the Market Place at the corner with Newbegin. Still there today but here showing Mr. Barr's trade of Plumber, Glazier and Painter. An assortment of windows on the first floor include eight-paned, six-paned and single-paned sashes.

Robert Walker, tinsmith, outside his shop at 5 Southgate in 1895. Robert Walker's family kept this shop until 1959. The tinsmith worked in sheet metal and made many essential kitchen utensils. Hornsea had several shops like this where one could buy hard soap, candles, lamp oil hardware, tinware, enamel utensils, oil lamps, lamp glasses and wicks – items rarely used nowadays. The tinsmith had a workshop behind his shop where he repaired leaking kettles and pans and made hardware of all shapes and sizes to order. Mass-produced enamelled goods were beginning to appear and some are on display in the window.

Mr. Barr's shop in later years. It is a fine building standing on a prestigious site close to the Church and Market Place. The first floor windows are the same as those shown in the earlier picture on page 61 but the entire ground floor is now one large shop and the shop windows have been extended round the corner of the building. For many years it was William's outfitter's shop; after the war it was taken by Mrs. Elsie Shaw and became a hardware and china store.

This was the holiday home run by the Guild of Brave Poor Things. This Hull-based charity maintained the home in New Road, Hornsea, just a few hundred yards from the sea. The Home was used to give long-term disabled people a holiday by the sea. Although this picture was taken in 1904, the charity was still at work after the Second World War.

Hornsea County Secondary School was built in the late 1950's on ground once occupied by the Hall in Eastgate. The Hall was the home of the Wade family from 1844-1897. The family timber business was based in Hull and the firm became the largest importer on the East Coast. The Wade family was a great benefactor to Hornsea and active in politics, education, and agriculture, and petitioned the government of the day on these and many other subjects. In addition to the brick and tile works at Hornsea the Wades had 400 acres of farm land under cultivation around the town, much of which is now built on. A fuller account of the Wade family can be found in the *Timber News and Saw Mill Engineer* of 7 March 1896. The main entrance to the school was once the main gate to the Hall.

Cromwell's Arch. This group of buildings in Southgate has long since gone. Half-way along the row an archway gave onto Grainger's yard. It is said that during the English Civil War, when the Parliamentary forces held Hull against the King, Oliver Cromwell's troopers rode into Hornsea and stayed at an Inn in the yard. What effect Cromwell's well-fed, well-trained and well-armed troopers must have had on the people of Hornsea can only be imagined, but the legend lives on. There is evidence that Cromwell's men defaced a tomb in the church.

This picture celebrates the laying of the foundation stone of the Hornsea War Memorial Cottage Hospital on 12 October 1922. The chairman of the committee was Mr Collinson and members of his committee were Mr S. Earl and Mr J. Hornsey (not in this photograph). In the picture are; back row, left to right: J.T. Levitt, builder; A. Clark, stonemason; F. Smith, labourer; F. Myers, joiner; -?-, bricklayer; -?-, apprentice; H. Onions, bricklayer; W. Robinson, foreman joiner; D. Knaggs, labourer; -?-, architect. Middle row: H. Adkin, foreman bricklayer; ? Jarvis, joiner; F. Harland, joiner; F. Grantham, bricklayer; C. Grantham, bricklayer; W.Russell, labourer; J. Brown, labourer; J. Hood, labourer. Front row: F. King, plumber; -?-; W. Jackson, labourer; -?-, apprentice. The photograph was taken by Mr C. Porter who was an apprentice on the job. Money to build the hospital was raised by subscription as a memorial to those who fell in the First World War. It has been extended over the years and is greatly valued by the people who live in the town today.

This is the windmill that served Cherry and Wade's brick and tile works at the top of Marlborough Avenue. These works are where the Hornsea Pottery factory is today. The Mill was a six-storeyed tower mill with five sails and was used to provide motive power for the works. The house and the buildings in the background remain today but the mill has disappeared and only the clay pond is left to remind us of the old works.

This is Hornsea's other windmill, in 1900, the Mill that ground the corn for the people of Hornsea. It was a fine example of a six-storey brick tower mill. The picture shows the set of four sails with horizontal shutters. These shutters were automatically adjusted to keep the sails turning at an even speed, which was essential to operate the two pairs of massive grinding stones. This mill, like many others, was overtaken by technology. Steel rolling mills took over corn milling and at the same time small portable oil engines were imported into the country enabling farmers to do most of the mill's work on the farm. So these graceful windmills fell into disuse.

This is the impressive colonnaded entrance to Hornsea Town railway station in its heyday. Until the closure of the railway the entrance remained much the same as when first built, even retaining the rings set into the pillars for tethering horses. Much of the building is still intact and has been skilfully incorporated in the houses and flats of Station Court.

Quaker Cottage. This very traditional cottage poses a quaint paradox. Its back door is on the front in Westgate, and its front door is on Back Westgate. The front elevation shows two doors with raised steps and three Yorkshire slide windows. The lower part of the front wall is buttressed by extra courses of cobbles giving added strength to the wall. The garden at the rear is enclosed by a cobbled wall. On the roadway at the near corner of the cottage is a large whitewashed boulder put there when the cottage was built to deter vehicles from cutting the corner and damaging the walls.

Six

The Early Seafront
and the Pier

THE SANDS. HORNSEA.
FIFTY YEARS AGO.

This is the view to the north taken from the deck of Hornsea's ill-fated Pier. The houses on the left are now part of Marine Drive. There are about eight bathing machines on the sands, four are at the water's edge in use and four are further up the beach awaiting customers. In the distance to the right is the old Marine Hotel. The old building was demolished about 1900 and the present hotel built on the same site.

The Promenade Gardens looking south towards the new Marine Hotel. The gardens were laid out on the north cliff to commemorate the Diamond Jubilee of Queen Victoria. The money to pay for this work was raised by public subscription. There is no protection from the sea. This is where the first sea wall was built in 1907.

This is an artist's impression of the old Marine Hotel of 1848 , showing a building with more than sixteen chimneys. A building of truly great proportions is shown with its own private road to the beach. In 1900 a much smaller Marine Hotel was photographed being demolished!

The North Promenade c. 1904. The Marine Hotel has a flag flying and the band is playing. The seats and the shelters are full of people. On the distant beach beyond the bathing machines crowds throng the sands. It is probably a bank holiday and the crowds have come to Hornsea for the Regatta.

More happy holidaymakers enjoying the sea and the sands at Hornsea. All seem interested in the view and judging by the well-dressed crowd gathered on the wooden sea wall they are enjoying a Bank Holiday Regatta. A cameraman has set up his tripod in the centre of the crowd to record the scene.

The Promenade, c. 1903. In the bandstand the band is playing and people are strolling along enjoying the attractions of the promenade. In the distance, just behind the band stand, a white sheet is suspended on two long poles. This is a screen for an outdoor Bioscope show, (early moving pictures). This photograph was taken before the ill-fated Granville Court Hotel was built.

The Promenade, c. 1905. Children and dogs are being walked on the promenade. The gardens and promenade are an attraction for residents and visitors. The writer of this postcard tells a different story: "Dear Aunt Lucy [she writes] Mother wants to know if you are all still living. Mother thought you must be dead because you had not written, with Aunt Polly being away we never hear how you are, nor anything else. Hoping you are all well with love to Uncle and yourself from Gladys p.s Hope uncle is keeping alright now." The postage on a postcard in 1905 was one half penny. This was a cheap and reliable form of mass communication.

A peaceful corner near the promenade in the Floral gardens. Each year they were planted out with flowers to attract the visitors. Here, the flowers spell out HORNSEA FLORAL GARDENS. The seats and shelters are full of people enjoying the peace and tranquility.

There is a lot going on in this action-packed picture of Hornsea sands. The long, low building of Usher's Cafe dominates this part of the beach. There are swings and swing-boats and an aerial ropeway. It cost 6 old pence to have a go on the ropeway. First one climbed the steps to the platform, then threw the hanger over the wire which was suspended about 15 feet from the ground. Then, to a chorus of yells and encouragement, one launched oneself into space and flew across the beach to land on the far side. There are a score or more donkeys in the picture waiting for riders. There was a time when no visit to the seaside was complete without a donkey ride. Straw hats, sand in your shoes, and sunshine were all part of a day out.

The Hornsea Pier Company Plaque.

HORNSEA PIER FIFTY YEARS AGO

Mr. Wade's Hornsea Pier began its short life in controversy and ended in near tragedy. He hoped to build the Pier to compliment the opening of the railway on 28 March 1864. Early attempts were washed away by the sea and a rival of Mr Wade attempted to build a second pier 700 yards to the south. In 1878 , after many legal battles , Mr. Wade started to construct the pier on the original site but the work was beset by troubles and had to be completed by another firm. It was opened in May 1880. Hornsea had little time to admire its Pier for in October the same year a storm bound ship, the Earl of Derby, collided with it and some three hundred yards of the seaward end collapsed into the sea.

This is the view the visitor had from the deck of the Pier in 1880 showing the seating arranged along the sides of the Pier, and the gas lamps illuminating the structure. The Alexandra Hotel and the Congregational Church are prominent on the sky line. The lady walking on the Pier has her umbrella up.

This pen and ink sketch of the Pier and the ill-fated *Earl of Derby* shows the contemporary scene on the beach after the dreadful gale on the night of 30 October 1880. The vessel lost her sails and steerage during the night, and was driven towards the shore and crashed into the Pier demolishing the seaward end. All the details are in the picture, the ship, the lattice Pier, the collapsed trestles, and the wreckage on the beach. The Old Marine hotel is in the background and in the foreground is a sewer outfall pipe. When the wreck was reported local people turned out to rescue the crew. Fortunately there were no fatalities that night. The parish magazine reports that 'On Sunday 31 November a considerable number of the crew of the *Earl of Derby* went to church in Hornsea to give thanks for their merciful escape from death. The Vicar said a few words on the subject at the end of his sermon'. That was not to be the end of the story – for to the present day the Pier and the *Earl of Derby* still excite comment.

A view taken on the beach close to the damaged Pier. These appear to be screw piles which were used in the construction of the Pier. The screw end was driven into the sand and clay to support the structure. Alexander Mitchell, a blind engineer, invented the screw pile in 1835 and similar piles were used in the construction of light houses at Maplin Sands, Eddystone, and Belle Rock.

In 1979 a pipeline was being laid in a trench on the sea bed along a line approximately where the Pier had been. These two huge piles were recovered from the sea bed during that operation. These timbers with their screw ends were found in the same place as those shown in the previous picture of 1880. They must have been on the sea bed for nearly a hundred years. Two of the recovered piles are on display in the Town.

Low tide after the *Earl of Derby* had collided with the Pier. When the seaward end collapsed it made the whole structure unsafe and a light was fixed to the seaward end to warn shipping of the danger. Eventually the Pier was dismantled and most of the remains taken to the yard of Gabriel, Wade and English in Hull. During the 1950's the Pier Company's plaque was recovered from the salvaged timber.

After the Pier had been dismantled, all that remained was this building at the Pier head. It was used at various times as a store and a summer residence. Eventually the old building fell into disuse and no trace of it can be seen today. On the beach Hornsea fishing cobble No. H621 provides some shelter for the holiday makers.

Hornsea north cliff looking south towards the old Marine Hotel, *c.* 1890-95. In the distance is all that remained of the deck of the Pier after the debris from the *Earl of Derby*'s collision had been cleared away. The field and cliff top path in the foreground are where the Jubilee Gardens of 1898 and the sea wall and Promenade of 1907 were eventually built. The building of the Floral Hall in 1913 completed the first stage of the sea front as we know it today.

Seven

The Lifeboat and
the Gales

In 1857 the first R.N.L.I. lifeboat to be stationed at Hornsea was called the *B. Wood*. The work done and the lives saved by the *B. Wood* and her successors is recorded both in the church and in publications such as the *History of the Hornsea Lifeboat Station* by John D. Fox R.N.L.I. In the picture the boat is about to be launched by horses harnessed to the lifeboat carriage. The boat was driven off the carriage into the sea, a difficult job even in the best of weather. From the lifeboat house the horses pulled the lifeboat on its carriage through the town, onto the beach, and into the water until the boat could be launched from the carriage into the sea.

A group of some of Hornsea's fishermen, *c.* 1905. They worked the fishing cobbles in the background. Here, they and their children are dressed in their Sunday best. Their every-day working jerseys are drying on the gunwhale of the nearest cobble. The 'skeets' in the right foreground enabled a heavy boat to be launched from a sloping sandy beach. The boat slid along with the skeets under the keel either up or down the beach.

A yacht ashore at Hornsea. Although this yacht was floated off at high tide with little damage, it is a reminder of the dangers of the sea and the work of the lifeboats everywhere.

This stirring scene shows the recovery of the Hornsea lifeboat after a launch. Three pairs of farm horses with their handlers haul the heavy boat and carriage out of the sea and back to the lifeboat house. The lifeboat was housed in the building that is now Hornsea's town hall. A bell hung above the entrance and was rung to summon the lifeboatmen and the horses and handlers from nearby farms. The horse teamsters in the picture are, Josh Walker, Will Walker, Bob Brown and W. Banks. The carriage wheels were fitted with patent Boydall plates to prevent the heavy carriage sinking in the soft sand. The noise these plates made as they clattered on the road brought out the crowds to follow the lifeboat and watch the launch.

In Memoriam.

GEORGE PEARCE, AND RICHARD WITTY,
(Aged 26 Years)   FISHERMEN,   **(Aged 22 Years)**

DROWNED BY THE UPSETTING OF THEIR BOAT OFF HORNSEA BEACH,

At 10-0 a.m., on the 22nd November, 1887.

Three hardy Fishers launched their boat, this bleak November morn,
To haul their lines, and bait their hooks, regardless of the storm;
An arduous and precarious life the fisherman's must be,
And poor and scant in Winter time is the harvest of the sea.

This scanty harvest they had gained, then rowed towards the land,
But ere the kelson of their boat had touch'd the shingly strand,
A hungry giant billow leapt forth from Neptune's caves,
O'erturned their boat, retook their spoil, and plunged them in the waves.

Then in its greedy undertow embraced them with its might,
And drew them quick to unknown depths, far, far from human sight:
George Usher, whose tenacious grip held fast his trusty oar,
By its strong aid was buoyed afloat and carried safe to shore.

No aid could reach the two who strove this friendly shore to gain—
Encumbered by their huge sea dress their struggles were in vain.
Stern Death, exultant, held them fast—he knew these very men
Had robb'd him of his prey ful oft, and would do so again.

Yet He who holds the waters in the hollow of His hand;
Who weighs the hills in balances, and measures out the sand;
Who marks the lonely sparrow's fall, He, He alone can see
These Fishermen now lying dead, deep in the cold North Sea.

'Tis not in our weak finite sense to judge the ways of God,
But humbly bow our stiffenn'd necks beneath His chastening rod,
And pray that He may grant us light to see our duty clear,
To ease the widow's sore distress, and dry the orphan's tear.

          C. DIBBLIN.

Westgate, Hornsea, Nov. 25th, 1887.

SOLD FOR THE BENEFIT OF THE WIDOW AND FATHERLESS BOY OF THE ABOVE-NAMED GEORGE PEARCE.

This is a black band broad sheet published and sold on the streets for the relief of the family of George Pearse, drowned off Hornsea in November 1887. This was one of the ways that distressed families obtained help when the bread winner was lost. Although this incident took place over one hundred years ago similiar tragic accidents are still all too familiar wherever men go down to the sea in ships.

This wall plaque is in the parish church and on it is recorded the work carried out by the Hornsea lifeboats and their crews.

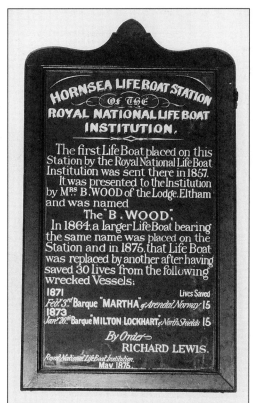

Gales and rough seas are no strangers to this shore as this incident of 13 February 1905 records. The Grimsby trawler *Drake* went aground below the cliffs at Mappleton, south of Hornsea. It is recorded that the new lifeboat, *Ellen and Margaret of Settle*, was launched to the aid of the trawler. The trawler skipper declined assistance and as the lifeboat left for home she capsized and all eleven crewmen were thrown into the sea. The boat quickly righted herself and all eleven crewmen regained the boat safely and returned to shore.

This picture was taken during a record high tide in March 1906. The seas are breaking over the old unprotected North Promenade. The boulder clay cliffs offered little resistance to heavy seas and were quickly eroded by storms such as this.

After the storm of 12 March 1906. The same scene after the tide had receded and the sea had calmed down. This was the damage sustained by the Promenade. Hornsea was not alone; widespread damage was reported all along the east coast of England.

Royal Commission on Coast Erosion at Hornsea.

After the severe battering this coastline received from storms and high tides at the beginning of the century, the damage was so great that a Royal Commission was formed to examine the whole problem of coastal erosion. Here we see the members of the Commission deliberating on the foreshore at Hornsea. Once again a small boy and a dog have joined the crowd.

Work began in 1906 to build a sea wall. The wall was to be 700 feet long, stretching from the north end of the beach to the Marine Hotel. Its foundations would be some 20 feet below the beach levels. In this photo the work on the foundations is well under way. The seaside donkeys are being used to carry the spoil away. The wall was made of armoured concrete and the total cost of the work was £10,500.

At the same time as the sea wall was being built a new convalescent home was erected nearby. The site was conveyed to the Trustees of the Victoria Hospital for Sick Children in Hull on very favourable terms from Mr. Christopher Pickering. The home cost £4,000 and most of the money was raised by public subscription. The foundation stone was laid on the same day as the new sea wall was officially opened to the public. The picture shows a garden party taking place at the home.

OPENING OF THE . . .

New Promenade and Sea Wall.

3.30   The Chairman of the Urban Council, Mr. C. E. A. Lyon, J.P., will introduce the Engineer, Mr. W. T. Douglass, C.E., to Mrs. A. Stanley Wilson.

3.40   Mrs. A. Stanley Wilson and the invited guests will proceed to the Promenade, and on the invitation of the Engineer

3.45   Mrs. Wilson will declare the New Promenade and Sea Wall open.

3.50   Proceed along the new Promenade to the Drinking Fountain, presented to Hornsea by Mr. W. T. Douglass, C.E.

3.55   Mrs. W. R. F. Collinson will unveil the Fountain.

4.0   Return to South Tennis Court.

4.5   Mr. J. H. Jackson will propose a vote of thanks to Mrs. A. Stanley Wilson.

4.10   Mr. A. Stanley Wilson, M.P., for Holderness, will reply and propose a vote of thanks to Mrs. Collinson.

43

The official opening of the new sea wall promised to be a grand affair. All the important people of the Town were there as well as many visitors. This timetable and list of proceedings is ample proof of the importance of the occasion.

Here the crowds of people are waiting under the waving flags and colourful bunting for the official declaration that the new sea wall is open. The ceremony was performed by Mrs. Wilson, the wife of Mr. Stanley Wilson, M.P. for Holderness. The tape was cut and the sea wall and promenade were declared open at 2.30pm on 6 July 1907!

At 3.55pm precisely that same afternoon another ceremony took place. Mr. W.R.F. Collinson unveiled the fountain, the gift to Hornsea by Mr. W.T.Douglas C.E., who was the engineer on the seawall project. Here is the exact moment for which the excited crowd has waited all afternoon. The boy with the camera, the man from the press, and the small dog are all part of the crowd.

This is the object of all the attention. The drinking fountain, which was presented to the people of Hornsea by the project Engineer to commemorate the opening of Hornsea's first sea wall. This same sea wall still protects the north promenade. The armoured concrete used in the construction of both the drinking fountain and the sea wall has stood the test of time. This photograph was taken between 1907, when the fountain was built, and 1913, when the Floral Hall and Granville Court Hotel were completed.

Eight

The Floral Hall,
New Sea Wall
and Beach

A view of the Promenade in 1914/5, which shows the improvements made possible after the building of the new sea wall. The lower and upper promenades are joined by flights of steps and slopes. Behind the promenade are the new gardens and the Floral Hall. The notice on the iron railings advertises an orchestral concert in the new hall. Behind the Floral Hall is the outline of the ill-fated Granville Court Hotel.

Inside the new Floral Hall a quartet plays to an empty hall. The ferns give a tropical air but the condensation problem must have been immense ! The Floral Hall was built after the fashion of the Crystal Palace, all glass and wrought iron.

HORNSEA. PROMENADE, LOOKING NORTH.

Here the full grandeur of the new North Promenade can be appreciated. This picture was taken from below the Marine Hotel and shows the upper and lower promenade and the Floral Hall. Behind is the tower and dome of the Granville Court Hotel.

This is the northern end of the beach, where the cliffs and sands are safer for both children and adults. Here a cross-section of holidaymakers smile for the camera. The boulder clay cliffs in the background contrast with the white changing tents which have been pitched on the beach.

Visitors on their way towards the Town railway station pass those making their way towards the beach on a sunny summer day. The flat roof of Brampton House can be seen in the background. This building was once a school but more recently has been divided into flats.

93

Near the beach the staff of the establishment known as Usher's Café wait for customers. There appear to be seventeen members of staff posing self consciously for the camera. This family business served refreshments to countless visitors over many years.

Usher's in later years. The old building burnt down and this was the replacement. It in turn suffered the same fate in later years. This letter head shows the date to be the 1930's.

Hornsea swimming club was established at the northern end of the promenade. The changing tents, the deck chairs and the club's tent are all under the watchful eye of the coastguard look out position on the cliff top.

This picture was taken from the high point on the south cliffs looking north along the sea front towards the Marine Hotel. In the distance is the group of holiday bungalows which developed into Pasture Road. This is a rare pre-war snapshot taken in the 1930's before the the boating lake and shelter were built behind this southern part of the promenade.

The boating lake and the shelter on the south promenade nearing completion. This was part of an extensive development on the seafront. Here Percy Harness, who was an electrician, and his mate Steve Parker are connecting up the electric lights round the boating pool. They were employed by the South-East Yorkshire Lighting and Power Company. In the foreground a stone mason and his mate are finishing off the stone work surrounding the pool. The boating lake, with its facilities for teas and refreshments, became popular with both residents and visitors. This all fell into disuse during the war as the sea front was out of bounds to the public. Sadly, the boating lake never regained its pre-war glory.

A post-war development on the sea front. This picture was taken from the top of the helter skelter. It was built by the local firm of Robinson and Prescott for W.E.Underwood and was opened in 1955 by the Chairman of the Hornsea U.D.C., Councillor Reg Brown. Bill Underwood and his family have been associated with the development of amusements and rides on the seafront since well before the war. The helter skelter remained until 1975. In the distance is Pickering's caravan site and Norman's farm.

The helter skelter and pleasure garden were on the north side of Sands Lane. This is very near the spot where the Pier stood. In the background to the left is the Town railway station. This picture was taken in 1964, the year that the railway closed for passenger traffic. From now on all the visitors would have to travel to Hornsea by road.

Donkeys at work on the beach. The animals look bored but their riders smile for the camera. These donkeys were farmed out to enthusiasts for the winter and during the summer lived in stables in the town. They trotted to the beach in the morning and returned along Newbegin in the late afternoon accompanied by a crowd of children.

This is a typical beach scene in the 1950's. Ice cream is on sale under the clock. On the beach, visitors sit on deck chairs behind wind breaks with their thermos flasks of tea. In the middle distance is the jetty which was built to help ferry visitors out to H.M.S *Duchess*. This was a Royal Navy destroyer which visited Hornsea as part of the Coronation celebrations on 2 July 1953. Afterwards the jetty was used by fishermen until it was eventually destroyed by the sea.

Nine

People at Work and Play

Whit Monday 27 May 1912 finds the local lads dressed in their Sunday best. They are wearing straw boaters, high collars, and an assortment of neck ties. They are carrying walking canes and have posies in their button holes as they parade outside the Parish church. On the extreme left of the group is the young Matt Quayle.

Hornsea Cricketers, 1905. The Gentlemen. Back row: H. Burnett, H. Whiting, T. Robinson, Mr Huscroft, G. Scott. Seated: H. Miskin, G. Hinch, J. Swales, Mr Parker, Mr Train, T. Hunger. On the ground: Mr. Jackson, Mr. Bulmer, Mr. Arksey. The small boy is not named.

Hornsea Cricketers, 1912. The Ladies. All eleven of the team pose for the photo. Front row, left to right: Mary Hornsey, Nora Marshall, Gwen Hampshaw (Captain), Marie Harrison, Miss Hargreave, Back row: -?-, Dorothy Stephenson, Miriam Cograve, Katie Lonsdale, Dorothy Trendle, Alex Wood.

Hornsea United Football Club, 1924. Winners of the Hospital Cup 1924. Back row, left to right: Fred Simpson, ? Billingham, George Loten (painter and decorator), Cyril Hall, (killed during the Second World War), George Dean, Mr. Hart, George Hall, Jos Harrison. Middle row: Phil Loten, Jimmy Nutt, Jack Taylor, Front row: Laurie Hart, Arthur Hebden, Ernest Carr, John Habbershaw, Sid Hood. The picture was taken on the football field on Hull Road.

Members of the Hornsea Ladies Hockey Club, 1908. Two of the ladies are wearing huge flat caps and the lady by the goal post has the Club mascot in her arms. No names are available for the team.

The opening of the scout headquarters on the sea front. The building was where Marine Drive now joins little Eastgate. It was one of a group that stood opposite the car park on Marine Drive and at right angles to the sea. Included in the parade are Eric Ballard, Bill Ballard, Mr. Lonsdale, and Walt Smith. The picture was taken in 1910. Robert Stephenson Smyth, 1st Baron Baden-Powell of Gilwell, had started the Boy Scout movement in 1908.

The Hornsea Girl Guides, probably around 1921. The only guides we can name with certainty are Rhoda Robson, who is sitting smiling on the left and Nellie Walker standing seriously on the extreme right.

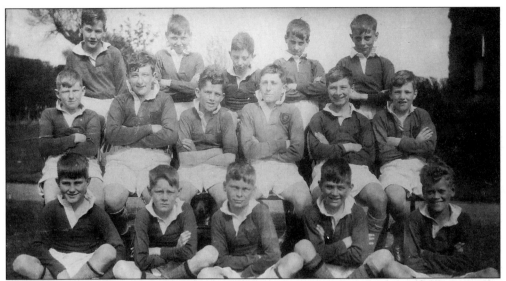

St. Bede's school rugby team, 1934/35. Back row, left to right: C. Fawcett, J. Hultum, J. Sims, R. Dawson, F. Kemp. Second row: J. Price-Jones, A. Beauteman, G. Brown, A. Loten, M. Cartledge, R. Strachan. Front row: M. Strachan, W. Barr, P. Carmichael, A. Brown,. R. Frost. St. Bede's was one of several private schools in Hornsea.

This De Dion Bouton of 1898 was photographed in Shuttleworth's garage in Alexandra Road. (Note the concrete block wall). The car belonged to Peter Gaskell of Hornsea. On this occasion Mrs. M.I. Hay, his daughter, is in the driving seat with her brother Reg beside her. In 1939 this same garage was advertising a day and night private ambulance service.

The Ladies of Hornsea at work. In 1954, members of the Women's Voluntary Services (the W.V.S.) demonstrate their skills and initiative by cooking a meal in the open air using a home-made field kitchen. The chimney of the oven is made from empty National Dried Milk tins. (photograph courtesy of *Hull Daily Mail*)

The Ladies of Hornsea at play. A tense moment during a game of bowls on the bowling green by the Floral Hall. The flat bowling greens of Victoria Gardens were once advertised as a feature of the Promenade entertainments. (photograph courtesy of *Hull Daily Mail*)

Floral Hall, Hornsea. Members of the Hornsea and District Chamber of Trade and their invited guests enjoying the annual dance held on the nearest Wednesday to St. Valentine's Day, 14th February, *c.* 1963. The fine maple dance floor of the Floral Hall had to be replaced after the heavy wear sustained during the war years, when dances in the hall were enjoyed by the many soldiers stationed in the town.

Travelling by bus to Hornsea in the early 1920's meant a ride on the Red Chara. Here on the cliff top at Hornsea is AT 7417 of the Newington Omnibus Co's fleet. It is a Crossley Ex-R.F.C. 14-seater, licenced in Hull as No. 131. The Red Chara ran to Hornsea from Hull via Beverley and the fare was 2s 6d. If it started to rain the driver would stop and the passengers help him put up the hood. The kiosk in the background was run by a Miss Loten.

During the Boer war, Lord Baden-Powell defended the town of Mafeking until the seige was relieved on 21 May 1900. This military event was widely celebrated in this country. In Hornsea the school celebrated the victory by building this large sand-castle on the beach. The castle was topped by a Union Jack and the words BADEN-POWELL MAFEKING were picked out in white pebbles.

Hornsea Council School celebrates soon after its opening in 1935. This may have been Empire Day. At one time schools always celebrated Empire Day, and in Hornsea pupils sang 'Empire Day, Twenty-fourth of May, If you don't give us a holiday, we'll all run away.' Empire Day celebrated Queen Victoria's birthday and was widely observed as a school holiday. The day commemorated the assistance given to the mother country by the colonies in the South African wars, 1899-1900.

This is a rare picture of the 10.5 inch gauge model railway line on the sea front at Hornsea. The locomotive was a Bassett-Lowke North Eastern Atlantic 4-4-2. The three four-seater coaches had glass end screens. The train ran on a circular track with a footbridge and station. The line was operated for a few years in the early 1930's but had left Hornsea by 1936.

Hornsea Fire Engine. John Barr, plumber and decorator, used to have an old Ford motor car with a trailer. When there was a fire, out went the plumber's tools and in went the fire fighting equipment. The car often had to be push-started. This picture records the inauguration of Hornsea's first motor fire engine, *c.* 1925. John Barr became Captain of this engine.

A picture of three retired gentlemen of Hornsea relaxing, sitting on a wall. From left to right are: Mr William Buttimer, Mr. William Bennett Stephenson, and Mr. Ben Bolton, who was the father of B.C. Bolton who played cricket for Yorkshire in the 1890's.

This is Mr. William Buttimer, who spent a long and distinguished career in the Royal Navy. For this he was awarded the Long Service and Good Conduct Medal. The picture shows him wearing the medal. After leaving the Navy he joined the coastguards at Hornsea.

Another well-known face around the streets of Hornsea. Jim Hartley, who delivered milk twice daily for most of his working life. He is seen here as a young man with his carrier bike. This was in the days when milk came in churns and was ladled out in half- or one-pint amounts into the customer's milk jug.

Jim Hartley delivering milk in his horse drawn milk float in Southgate. He was a familiar sight in the town from the 1930's, when this photograph was taken, until well into the 1970's. By that time bottles, sterilisation and refrigeration had taken over from the horse-drawn float and the milk churn.

These two errand lads are seen outside the Bonnet Box in Newbegin on 20 May 1934. The boy on the left is Peter Bradley. Many people will remember the whistling errand lads doing their Saturday morning jobs of delivering goods from the shops to customers all over town. This form of delivery is rarely seen today. There was a time when all telegrams were delivered by smartly dressed Post Office telegram boys speeding along on their bikes.

Peter Bradley, the errand boy in the previous picture, joined the Royal Navy. He is second from the left, second row down in Class 234 Royal Arthur. After he qualified as a communications telegraphist, his wartime service took him to the U.S.A. on convoy duties. He then had a spell of duty aboard aircraft carriers with the Home Fleet and later travelled to other parts of the world. When Peter left the Navy he joined the Coastguards and served with distinction for many years. He brought his telegraphy skills to 'civvy street' as an accomplished amateur radio operator.

This is Mr. Squire with one of Mr. William Robinson's cart horses, pictured in 1905. These heavy horses did all the haulage work long before the invention of the steam and petrol engine. The medium waggon in the background carries Mr. Robinson's name and trade. Many individual skills and crafts were needed before a waggon could be completed and ready for a lifetime of work.

A bit of old Hornsea in 1912, the cottage (second doorway) where Mr. Carrier Robinson lived and from where he ran his business. The board on the wall reads W. ROBINSON. HULL AND HORNSEA CARRIER. Next door was where Mr. T. Garton, boot and shoe maker, lived and worked. These cottages were demolished to make way for the building of King Street off Southgate. King Street provided access when Southgate Gardens was built in 1922.

For many years the Hornsea Ex-Servicemen's Club held a flower show in the grounds of the Hornsea Urban District Council's offices in Elim Lodge on Cliff Road. The show was held on August Bank Holiday Monday and people came from miles around to exhibit or to admire. Of all the Hornsea folk here, the one who can be named is Matt Quayle, who has his back to the camera.

Matt Quayle, 1955. This was taken during Matt's time as a rat catcher. He was a Manxman who came to Hornsea as a youth and spent the rest of his life here. He started work as a butcher's boy and eventually owned his own butcher's shop. During the First World War he and his mate Bill Banks served in Salonika working with a mule train. Before coming home they sold all their clothes and spare kit and bought a vast quantity of cheap Greek tobacco. Matt was a familiar figure at local cattle markets and he enjoyed following the Holderness Hunt. Matt's yard and garden in Southgate have now been built on but his name lives on as Quayles Mews. Matt is shown here with his Jack Russell terrier, Tiny, who was his constant companion.

The old Marine Hotel was demolished at the beginning of the century. It was dangerously close to the cliff edge and there was no protection from the sea until the sea wall was built in 1907. Alongside the old building the new Marine Hotel is taking shape. In the foreground, also very close to the cliff edge, is Mr. Shipley's set of Steam Gallopers ready for business. A wisp of steam rises from the funnel in the centre of the ride and all is set. The wheeled water cart nearby kept the thirsty steam engine supplied with water.

Father and son. The picture was taken near one of a line of huts that once stood on the south side of Sands Lane near the sand dunes. The huts were traditionally used by Hornsea fishermen to keep their bait and tackle in. This hut housed a 16-ft Norwegian dory called *Eucaliptus* which was used for fishing off the beach. Small boats such as these were often brought back from Scandinavia as deck cargo on the regular freighter runs of the time. The huts were demolished in the 1960's to make way for sea-front improvements.

113

Hornsea around 1946/47. Many of the hundred or so people in the picture took part in money raising efforts during the war years. Vast sums were collected during 'Spitfire', 'Salute the Soldier' and 'Warship' weeks. These very patriotic events were supported by hard-working local people who organised the events. This picture may well have been taken at the end of a very successful whist drive. The lady on the right is carrying her prize.

A fine picture of a holiday group taken on the sands at Hornsea. It is a wonderful study in the fashion of the day. Sailor suits for the boys, straw hats for the ladies, and bowler hats and walking canes for the gentlemen. The timber sea defences in the background suggest this was at the north end of the beach.

Marlborough Avenue, 1870. This magnificent five-sailed windmill was sited at the brick and tiles works of Messrs. Wade and Cherry. This factory was at the top end of Marlborough Avenue, and adjacent to the railway line. The mill pumped water from the clay pit and provided power to drive machinery. Although the mill has long gone the buildings are still there as part of the Hornsea Pottery Company's factory. Note the industrial windows.

One hundred years have passed since the last photograph was taken. Here, in 1970, Tommy Smith supervises the recovery of a clay truck from the clay pond of the old brick and tile works. The truck was probably dumped in the pond when the old works closed. Tommy Smith always opened the gates for the Pottery in the morning and was there to close them every evening. One morning the gates remained unopened – Tommy Smith had died.

The Hornsea Pottery factory. From the old clay truck in the previous picture to this modern truck about to enter the new, gleaming continuous rapid firing pottery kiln. This kiln reduced the firing time from 16 hours to less than 6 hours. It was the first tunnel kiln in this country to be fired by natural gas. The up-to-date interior contrasts sharply with the 1870 picture of the brick yard.

The Hornsea Pottery factory. Fitting the handles to the mugs before the glazing and firing process takes place.

The Hornsea Pottery factory, outside the main offices. In 1978 this international gathering of pottery manufacturers' representatives met at the Hornsea factory. Delegates came to this design conference from the U.S.A, Portugal, Colombia, and South Africa – such was the world-wide reputation of the Hornsea Pottery Co.

The Hornsea Pottery won major design awards for their work with Contrast, Concept and Ebony pottery. In this picture Colin Rawson receives the design awards from H.R.H Prince Philip at the Barbican Centre in 1980.

117

THE MODERN ARMY

A MECHANIZED COLUMN will move through the Counties of LEICESTERSHIRE, DERBYSHIRE, NOTTINGHAMSHIRE, LINCOLNSHIRE, YORKSHIRE (East & North Ridings)

Between JULY 24th and AUGUST 14th, 1938.

Most spectacular and comprehensive. The Mechanized Army with its swift movement (passing of the horse) will be demonstrated by Units of the :—

ROYAL ARTILLERY (Medium Artillery and Anti-Tank).
ROYAL ENGINEERS (Compressor Plant).
WIRELESS AND TELEPHONE EQUIPMENT, ROYAL CORPS OF SIGNALS.
AN INFANTRY PLATOON.
MACHINE GUNS OF THE INFANTRY.
A MORTAR DETACHMENT.
LIGHT AID DETACHMENTS.
ROYAL ARMY ORDNANCE CORPS.
TRAVELLING KITCHENS.

The Weapons to be shown include :—
MEDIUM ARTILLERY GUNS, NEW ANTI-TANK GUN, NEW ANTI-TANK RIFLE, BREN GUN, VICKERS GUNS, M.L. MORTAR.

The Column will comprise a strength of about 10 Officers and 190 Other Ranks and some of the latest types of maintenance and transportation vehicles.

DEMONSTRATIONS.

24th, 25th and 26th July, at 7-30 p.m.	-	Glen Parva Barracks, South Wigston, LEICESTERSHIRE.
28th July, at 7-30 p.m.	-	Bass Recreation Ground, DERBY.
29th July, at 7-30 p.m.	-	Queen's Park Annexe, CHESTERFIELD.
31st July, at 3-30 p.m.	-	Forest Recreation Ground, NOTTINGHAM.
2nd August, at 7-30 p.m.	-	Wyndham Park Recreation Ground, GRANTHAM.
4th and 6th August, at 7-30 p.m.	-	Camp, Wainfleet Road, SKEGNESS.
7th August, at 7-30 p.m.	-	Sidney Park Extension, CLEETHORPES.
8th August, at 7-30 p.m.	-	Camp Site, Station Road, SCUNTHORPE.
9th August, at 6-30 p.m.	-	Fair Ground, HULL.
10th August, at 4 p.m.	-	Sands Lane Car Park, HORNSEA.
11th August, at 4 p.m.	-	Bessingby Field, BRIDLINGTON.
13th August, at 12-15 p.m.	-	Show Field, WHITBY.
13th August, at 6-30 p.m.	-	Camp Field, REDCAR.

This programme advertises a visit to Hornsea by a mechanised army column on 10 August 1938. This programme was to demonstrate and show off the new British army. The modernisation and expansion of the armed forces had been accelerated by events in Europe.

On the beach, Hornsea, 1938. The mechanised rifle section is wearing steel helmets, battle dress and webbing equipment in the 15cwt truck – ready for action.

On the beach, Hornsea, 1938. Two motor cycle dispatch riders (Don R's) pause to take in their surroundings during the Army's visit. In the background are the swings and the aerial ropeway of the amusements on the beach.

On the beach, Hornsea, 1938. Small boys swarm all over the army's light tanks. Few would realise that within a year these troops would be mobilised on a war footing. Meanwhile on the sunny sands they have time to relax and show off.

This is a not such a mobile piece of ordnance. George William Clark and Sgt. Major Young have the breech block open to service this piece at the Drill Hall, Hornsea (the ex-servicemen's club), in 1906/7

To celebrate the Coronation of the Queen in 1953, this Destroyer paid a courtesy visit to Hornsea under the command of Captain H.R. Law, O.B.E., D.S.C. The public were invited to visit the ship, and the specially built jetty (see page 98) was used to ferry sightseers in fishing cobbles out to the vessel. Comments in a lady's diary of the time read, '17 June. H.M.S *Duchess* anchored off shore. Sailors all over the place!'

The beach, Hornsea, c. 1918. This De Haviland DH6 patrol aircraft just didn't make it back to its landing ground at Atwick. During the First World War these Atwick-based aircraft were used on anti-submarine duties and each carried a small bomb.

The cliffs, Hornsea. This Hawker Fury, probably from nearby Catfoss aerodrome, came to grief on the cliff top at Hornsea sometime in the early 1930's. The RAF and the local police cordoned off the aircraft and it was eventualy recovered and taken back to its base. This photograph was taken with a box brownie camera through a hole in a shopping bag by a local man!

Hornsea coastguards on mobilisation in 1939. All nine men are armed with rifles and some are carrying ammunition pouches. Many of these men are wearing medal ribbons awarded in earlier conflicts. Their intimate knowledge of the coastal area was invaluable to the military authorities during the Second World War.

A church parade and thanksgiving service held in 1903/4 for the safe return of men from the Boer Wars. Five men of the East Yorkshire Yeomanry went to South Africa and five came home safely.

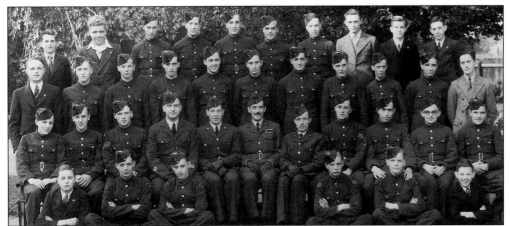

The Air Training Corps was founded on 5 February 1941. Later that year No. 298 Hornsea squadron was formed. The A.T.C. trained young men with the idea of pre-service training and later on most of these young men were called up into the armed forces, but not necessarily into the R.A.F. Back row: ? Ives, ? Bullock, A. Young, ? Usher, N. Medforth, G. Norman, -?-, R. Easterbrook, A. Montgomery, -?-. Second row: B. Vickerton, -?-, G. Hornby, R. Kemp, D. Davies, R. Thorndyke, -?-, ? Newton, J. Bird, R. Hampson, -?-. Third row: Ron Jordan, Ray Jordan, C. Varley, ? Rawson, ? Binnie, ? Machin, ? Bonner, A. Tabor, A. Addey, W. Binning. Front row: A.C. Peers, E. Train, C. Wright, K. Habbershaw, L. Sutton, J. Jobey. Roy Thorndyke must have joined up very early, for his National Enrolment Number was 12.

The visit of King George VI and Queen Elizabeth to inspect the coastal defences in wartime Hornsea in August 1940. The royal couple are on the promenade by the car park entrance to the Marine Hotel. The troops, all at attention, are guarding the naval gun in its camoflaged emplacement. The gun is heavily sandbagged. Whether the gun was ever fired either in practice or in anger is not recorded, but if it had been the noise would have been heard all over Hornsea. Our gun was one of a battery forming part of the defence of the Humber estuary and the coast of Holderness. A gunner major who lived in Hornsea as a young man and was posted to the battery at nearby Spurn Point said after the war that he felt as though he was personally defending his own back garden against Adolf Hitler!

The children of Hornsea Mereside school in the late 1920's. They are a healthy, happy bunch of children. In 1936, when the new school in Newbegin opened, the seniors and juniors transferred to the new school. The infants' school on Seaton Road then closed and the pupils were moved to Mereside School.

Here are the senior pupils at Hornsea Mereside school a year or so before they moved to the new school in Newbegin. Mereside was a Victorian school with no electricity, high windows, and primitive sanitary arrangements. The new Council School building was severely modern in design. It had a science laboratory, facilities for domestic science and woodwork, a children's library, and an assembly hall equipped for drama and film projection. It was surrounded by spacious play grounds, a large playing field and gardens, and must have impressed both pupils and teachers.

A photograph of some of the pupils of Hornsea school taken on 1 July 1898. The teacher, Mr. Sykes, can be seen on the left of the picture. Pupils identified are Frank, Charles and Harry Walker and Annie Bulson.

This photograph was taken on the steps of the south door of St. Nicholas' Church in October 1973. The Vicar, The Rev. John de Beverley Batemen, and the members of the church choir pose in the autumn sunshine. Left to right, back row: Peter Hall. Michael Smith. Howard Parker. Reg Anderson, Alec Richardson, Bill Browning. Second Row: Peter Tanton, Bill Kelsey, Rev. W.D. Hopkinson, Rev. J. de Beverley Bateman, John Boxall, Chris Mallon. Next row: Ashley Smith, Sarah Parker, Victoria Webster, Sarah Fairweather, Next row: Alison Browning, Giles Silcocks, John Webster, Helen Browning, Mark Rhodes, Nick Tanton, Roger Andrews, Philippa Wildgoose. Front row: Katy Barlow, Hilary Andrews, Alison Smith, Andrew Cooper, Elizabeth Tanton, Simon Rhodes.

This delightful picture postcard shows a father and his three children on the beach at Hornsea. They are dressed in their Sunday best for their visit to the seaside. The card is postmarked 8pm on 13 October 1908 and stamped by the Hull sorting carriage which formed part of the mail train.

This is a wedding photograph taken outside the Hornsea Primitive Methodist Chapel in the Market Place. The families and guests have assembled on the steps of the chapel with the wedding party after the ceremony. The date is about 1935.

Hornsea carnival. A patriotically decorated horse-drawn cart sets out to join the carnival procession in 1924. Although popular in the 1920's, the carnival lost support and had ceased to exist well before the Second World War. It was revived during the 1960's and has gone from strength to strength. It is now a three-day event and a highlight of the summer season.

Hornsea Town railway station, 17 October 1964. A small crowd of interested onlookers have gathered to watch the last regular Hornsea–Hull passenger train depart. A mourning wreath is hung on the locomotive's coupling.

Jeremiah Lamplough. This serene old gentleman was a postman around Hornsea for all of his working life. He was over 70 years old when this portrait was taken and at that age he was still walking his round to collect and deliver the mail. He is dressed for the job. From his highly-polished boots to his postman's hat he is ready for any weather.

Valediction. As a fitting end to this account of Hornsea a young lad waves good bye from the crowded beach by the Marine Hotel during the carnival in 1973.